ELEMENTAL
ELOQUENCE

Copyright © 2009 **Bradley Daniel Martin**

All rights reserved by the author. No part of this publication may be reproduced, stored in a retrieval system or transmitted in any form or by any means electronic, mechanical, photocopying, recording or otherwise, without the prior written permission of the author.

Cover Design by Caitlin Marie Hedrick

ISBN: 978-0-578-02797-5

PREFACE

Most of the poems and lyrics contained in this book, I believe, are words every person should live by. Everyone knows that cheating on your wife is bad. Everyone has sinned and thinks they can get away with it. We see too much poverty all over the world and yet do nothing about. We see wars come and go and sympathize with those left behind and grieve for the ones no longer with us. We see a child smile and then suddenly realize that it has brightened up our entire day and we are ready to face the world. We've also looked into the face of our own mortality and wondered about God. Most of the poems are of a serious nature and one, or two, might be humorous ... but they all are very poignant and have deep profound meaning. I challenge any one of you to not be moved by at least one of the poems in this book. Whether moved to tears or moved to laughter, my deepest hope is that this book sparks something.

DEDICATIONS

This book is dedicated to a soul that lovingly traversed this earth from January 27, 1952 - August 27, 2007. Thank you for making me part of your journey.

I LOVE YOU, MOMMY

TABLE OF CONTENTS

1. SMILES
2. LOVE SONG
3. SIN
4. WORDS
5. I LOVE YOU
6. SEARCHING FOR LOVE
7. HIDING
8. PATH OF LIFE
9. NIGHTMARES
10. DIFFERENCES
11. GRIEF
12. BEST GIFT
13. THING
14. LIVING WITH IT
15. MIXING RELATIONS
16. A CHILD'S LOVE
17. ADDICTION
18. FOR ELVIRA
19. BELIEF
20. BLEEDING LOVE
21. FOREVER
22. RELATIONSHIP BATTLE
23. POVERTY
24. HOW COME
25. FOR JOEY
26. MILITARY BRATS
27. CRUELTY
28. FOR CLINT
29. GIVE AND TAKE
30. ODE TO A SICK FRIEND
31. FOR MY SISTER
32. LIFE'S CRUTCH
33. PICK UP POEM
34. WAR
35. TREELESS
36. WHERE
37. RACE
38. DEATH
39. GOD STRUGGLE
40. THE GOOD & THE EVIL
41. MISSING MOM
42. WAR CRY
43. LIFE SEARCH
44. MASKED
45. UNITED OR DIVIDED
46. PATH OF SPIRIT
47. MOM'S GONE
48. OWN UP
49. FRIEND OR FOE
50. WHERE TO GO
51. DOWN
52. MY FAULT
53. HELP TO HEAL
54. REVELATIONS
55. SOUL SEARCHING
56. FINDING MY WAY
57. LOST LOVE
58. SCOTTY'S POEM

SMILES

Walking through the aisles
of my local grocery store
I cast my eyes on something
that I needed more than more

it wasn't a food item
or something artificial
it was very real
and one hundred percent special

what I saw as I was
making my way across the tile
was something that tugged my heartstrings
it was a child's smile

although I smiled first
the point I'm trying to make
is that a smile is better
than a German chocolate cake

a smile can do more
for a person's soul
than anything can do
that you put into your bowl

a smile can do more
to ease painful travesties
and unlike a bowl of candy
won't give you any cavities

smiles can do more
to ease a person's mind
than anything inside
a watermelon rind

smiles are more contagious
than any cold or flu
if you are so inclined
to give one, then please do

a smile can do more
to brighten a person's day
than anything you buy
with your weekly pay

smiles are really what
makes the world go around
but a greedy person thinks
money is where it's found

but my greed is for smiles
it's true I can't get enough
when a person smiles
I find I'm not so tough

a smile breaks through the walls
of any hardened heart
and causes just a little
of softening to start

smiles can turn a grinch
into a gentle man
and unlike so many laws
smiles they can not ban

so if you have a chance
when you see someone sad
just flash them a smile
and maybe they won't feel bad

smile is a word
that I like very much
and it is less intrusive
than a kindly touch

for fears and times have changed
as some hearts walk the lonely mile
but maybe they will cool
it starts with just a smile

LOVE SONG

Shine a light inside my heart
so my love can truly start
bring the words outside of me
and teach my soul just how to be

the love you have can be mine
I no longer have to whine
about the love I can't seem to find
now that you're here inside my mind

CHORUS
love is a part of life
and it can not be bought
but it's not instinctive
for it must be taught

I have loved and lost before
'til you knocked upon my door
now I will never lose again
the love I thought I couldn't win

when you took hold of my hand
you told me just where to stand
my heart no longer does it pine
because I know now that you are mine

CHORUS

I'm no sucker nor a chump
but my throat filled with a lump
when you said you loved me
now my heart can truly see

I'm no longer blind to what
my heart won't ever let me forget
that I feel the same way too
oh my darling, I love you

SIN

People say when you sin
you know you won't win
since I've been on this earth
I've seen sinning since birth

I've seen people pay
in a major way
I've seen people set free
on a major sinning spree

I wonder why there's no
rhyme or reason
to who is set free
and who's booked for treason

people say it's the rich
and the famous that prosper
but I've another very good
reason to offer

it's when we die
and hear the final bell
when we find out
who goes to heaven or hell

for in the end it's god
who decides our fate
so stop the sinning
before it's too late

or you'll be condemned
for an eternity unpleasant
an ever repeating thanksgiving day
where you are the holiday pheasant

WORDS

Words come
words go
how they affect
you never know

words can affect
everyone they touch
words can help
or hurt so much

good words can really
help one's self-esteem
bad words invade
the consciousness stream

evil words can tear
apart a person's mind
positive ones
leave something better behind

the words, "I love you"
can fill a person with love
while saying, "I hate you"
can mess with above

In the brain and the mind
these words do seep
and they can often affect
how one does sleep

words can give nightmares
or fill your dreams with light
no matter which words you choose
the wrong, or the right

so before you speak
pick wisely the words you choose
for it can make the difference
whether you win or you lose

for if positive words
are in fact what you speak
then later in life
your body won't leak

if negative words
come out of your mouth
you might find yourself
traveling south

A gun was toted by one
who heard a negative word
the shot rang out
"bang" is all that you heard

so make your words positive
with your very last breath
because negative ones
might lead to an early death

I LOVE YOU

I know that you care
I can see it everywhere
when you give me the support that I need
when people hurt me and make my heart bleed

but of all the things you say and do
it seems the hardest thing to say is "I love you"
that's all that I want and everything I desire
those three little words can set my heart afire

why is it so hard to say the thing I long to hear
I don't care how it's said, say it out loud or softly in my ear
just say those words once and let me know that you care
for my heart it is breaking and I'm in a pit of despair

CHORUS
I love you so much
but all we do is to touch
you never reach on the inside
you hang on to your selfish pride
can't say the words
though I know that you do
you can't bring yourself
to say "I love you"

I feel that there's nothing more that we can do
there's nothing left for us to hold on to
we used to be so good together you and I
now there's nothing to fight for, no reason to try

all our hopes and our promises, were they just a lie
did we come this far to just watch them die
all that I needed was three words so I'd stay
can't you just say them and not treat me this way

those magical words that fill a persons heart
when left unsaid really tear me apart
the words that would have bound us forever like glue
why couldn't you say it, because, I love you

CHORUS

and now we have parted, angry words often fail
to say what we mean, what our hearts long to tell
though we did try, in the end we were wrong
tried to make it happy, but ended with a sad song
the next one you meet, say this and be true
please don't leave me, because I love you

SEARCHING FOR LOVE

When life treats you bad
and you don't like what you've had
just heed my warning
wake up to a new morning

the next day is always new
fresh with glistening morning dew
as you open the door
to go out to the store

to find what you need
to make you heart bleed
when you find that special someone
who can help you turn the light on

keep a hold of them firm
and don't try and squirm
they show a sign
for they do pine

for what they've had before
show them what's in store
they just don't know
how to open up and show

the heart that's inside
because they try and hide
they've been hurt before
then shoved out the door

you know that feeling
because your heart is also reeling
now with a knife in their back
its confidence they lack

you must be the one
to show how it's done
forget yourself for the moment

and let your feelings lie dormant

concentrate on the task at hand
this is where your heart should land
this is where you want to be
stop saying "it's all about me"

work on the other one first
before their heart does burst
and they will find what their heart does miss
and you will finally live in bliss

HIDING

Feeling like you're shoved
inside a tiny box
with people outside laughing
you wish you had some rocks

to throw at them for labeling
you as this or as that
they can't see inside
to see where you heart is at

you are now stuck with this label
given a part to play
don't want more confusion
so you do it anyway

you want to tear the box down
and live the life you want
but you keep seeing familiar faces
the ones that want to taunt

faces from back then
right up until today
won't leave you alone
let the kid inside you play

they are with you always
even while you sleep
but others don't see the scars
they don't see you weep

for the boy you were then
and the man you have become
to them they seem the same
but they don't realize you're numb

there's something in your soul
way down deep inside
that keeps eating away at you
and will not let you hide

can't look into your eyes
and see the hidden flame
the burning eats you up
the beast you can't contain

try your best to keep it hidden
from everyone in sight
for if you were to let it out
they would scream in fright

they don't see that you have changed
from what you were before
they refuse to take your key
and open up the door

the window to your soul
although not crystal clear
is begging to be understood
and will not disappear

there's two entities inside you
both fighting for a prize
to show the world outside
what's hidden behind your eyes

your outward appearance normal
inside a war's occurring
others don't see the good and bad
line for you is blurring

you've played a game for so long
and others didn't know
but you're afraid the game is over
and the hidden "you" will show

don't want to show that hidden self
you're afraid what it will be
is it really acceptable
or will people just reject me

treat me as an outcast
and toss me to the side
that is why I can't come out
that is why I hide

I will let nobody in
because it is too late
and keep playing the role I have
and just accept my fate

the shell that is around me
the one that I've been living in
is way to comfortable for me now
it's like a second skin

PATH OF LIFE

Living your life your own way
not thinking of a consequence
taking a look back
would it have made a difference

what if I had listened
to the others before
would my life have equaled
a much bigger score

what if I had not done
what I did that day
would my life have turned out
a totally different way

I'm living in the present
always thinking of the past
could things have been different
who should I have asked

what should I have done
to be free from the now
I didn't ask the right questions
what, when, where, or how

my past will always be with me
flashing little reminders in my head
and sometimes come in nightmares
when I'm sleeping in my bed

when I wake up and realize
that's what I was before
I need knowledge quickly
to open another door

I do not wish to repeat
what knocked me to the ground
I've come to the conclusion
to turn my life around

instead of looking back
and resigning myself to fate
I should look forward
and realize it's not too late

I can't change what was
or what might have been
but I shouldn't have to lose
what I thought I couldn't win

I know I can do better
I will do my very best
because I finally found out
that I am truly blessed

NIGHTMARES

The nightmares I have
really get my goat
some make me want
to slit my throat

some honestly
really aren't all bad
some really make
me feel so sad

it's true that you never
forget what you've been through
but when the night comes
I really don't want to

live through again
what I've put behind me
but at night it comes back
to bite me in the hiney

a sudden flash, a picture
of times that weren't great
the nightmares come often
and seal my fate

I'm destined to have
a nightly return
of days gone by
that I wish I could burn

wipe out of my memory
for I can not
but those memories within me
really hurt an awful lot

sometimes I wake up
in a panic and screams
for I didn't have one
but a dozen bad dreams

of nightmares that make
me shiver or sweat
is the nightmare over
can I go back to bed yet

can I get the beauty sleep
I so richly deserve
or is another nightmare
going to grate on my nerve

there really is no lesson
if there is, then it's unclear
every night I fall asleep
I live in constant fear

but I know the next day
I'll wake up and adjust
to the day before me
I find that I must

if I let the nightmare
beat me and win
I'll surely be dead
and the devil will grin

if the last line of this poem
to you sounds odd
make no mistake
I believe in god

DIFFERENCES

Life is a strange
and beautiful thing
sometimes it makes you
want to get up and sing

sometimes you feel
like you're in a slump
and all you are good for
is lying there like a lump

sometimes you are so happy
that's how you make others feel
by just sharing your smile
you have mass appeal

there are many different opinions
and thoughts about this
is your life really doomed
or can you live in bliss

some say life is preplanned
something we should accept
other say their book isn't written
so that idea they reject

some say god has a plan
of which we cannot comprehend
other say if there were a god
surely the suffering would end

there are many people out there
all with different ideas in their mind
but the one thought that never differs
always try and be kind

people say that god loves
and forgives us all
there are other that believe

it's the size of the fall

one who has stolen or lied
can be forgiven
but one who has committed murder
must go to prison

people look on stealing and say
"give it back"
but for a more atrocious crime
they go on the attack

there is not one rule for some
different for some other
the only rule should be
respect and love each other

GRIEF

Grief can take on
many a different form
to some the way we grieve
can seem very cold or unusually warm

the important thing is
to grieve your own way
don't listen to anything
others have to say

like you have to cry
or you have to feel sad
when the fact of it is
you don't feel bad

it's not that you're callous
or that you are mean
it's just that others
haven't seen what you've seen

haven't been where you been
or seen through your eyes
they can't understand
that your grief is just lies

it's not that you're happy
or glad someone died
it's just hard to emote
though you have tried

some would see that
and say you're uncaring
but if you could cry
you wouldn't mind sharing

then others could see
the grief locked inside you
for though you can't show it
you feel as they do

BEST GIFT

Remember what I said
about gifts coming from the heart
and homemade gifts
are the best way to start

some people are not good
with their minds or their hands
so buying a gift at a store
is where the money lands

that doesn't mean that they
love you any less
this is the way they
choose to express

the feelings and the love
that they share for you
for they love you as equally
as I do

THING

The thing that I was
that I believed
was wrong on many levels
and poorly conceived

everyone I came across
thought I was a joke
my innocence lost
gone in a puff of smoke

they teased and they taunted
and did other mean things
how could these people
call themselves human beings

I was treated like an animal
figuratively locked in a cage
but I was too young
to understand all of my rage

with anger locked inside
a body so young
the backlash came out later
at the end of my tongue

said many hurtful things
and I didn't know why
some things were ugly
and caused others to cry

I didn't mean what I said
to cause others pain
but when I repeatedly spoke
I did it again

I've been trying to find
a way out for so long
that my mind gets mixed up
and doesn't know right from wrong

it's a tough learning process
to pull yourself out
from all of the anger
and the self doubt

just remind yourself always
that you are a human being
don't listen to the doubters
who once called you a thing

LIVING WITH IT

When we were young
you called it play
for what you made me
you must pay

I didn't really want
the memories I'm left with
surface life looks sweet
inside it's just a myth

these thoughts I have
don't feel like my own
they feel like their coming
from someone fully grown

someone able to grasp
onto the magnitude
of the differences between
respectable and lewd

I can not take back
things I did before
I can not forget
nor can I restore

the life that I once had
because now I'm fully grown
I have no one's protection
I feel I'm on my own

when thoughts creep back
into my mind
I feel that puts me
so far behind

the normalcy
that others had
I miss it now
I want it bad

I know I can't
spend my life
just thinking about
all of my strife

but it's hard sometimes
moving from the past
when you were taught
good times won't last

I feel that I can do it though
but it'll take some time
a good way to move on
is with a poem's rhyme

writing down your feelings
can help you regurgitate
the things that bring you down
and make you feel irate

and once you write your pain
and the stuff that makes you sad
you'll be able to concentrate
on feelings not so bad

like in the poem here
that started off real negative
once I wrote those feelings
I gave to them a sedative

and the bad feelings went away
and I stopped feeling sad
and then the only emotion
I had left was glad

MIXING RELATIONS

Mixing relations
mess up relations
 I tell ya mixing relations
 all they do is mess up relations

was goin' to a party
just the other night
hair was quaffed
pants skin tight

met this fine young girl
while driving down the road
she seemed so sad
I said "jump in, loosen that load"

got to the party
was havin' a little fun
saw somethin' strange
so I began to run

Got outta the car
the police said "hold it"
license and registration please
they thought I stole it

got home about
half past midnight
woke the girl up
she was ready for a fight

what she smelled first
was perfume in the room
she reached in a drawer
and I though "BOOM"

what she found next
was lipstick on my collar
I couldn't say nuthin'
she started to holla

she said "you know that party
and the girl with whom you messed
I knew you was mackin'
it was just a test

you proved to me
and my girls tonight
you're no man
you're just not right

the moral of this story
seems quite clear
you'll find located
in these words here

before you go out
and think you have a life
just remember
don't cheat on your wife

A CHILD'S LOVE

A child's love is the best love there is
a child's love is purest of them all
a child will still love you
when you begin to fall

a child's love is innocent
a child's love asks no questions
a child's love will give you no lies
or reasons to not trust them

CHORUS
children are the backbone of society
children are the reason that we care
without a child love in our lives
we will all be in constant despair

a child's smile lifts us up
a child's frown makes us weep
there is nothing more precious
then viewing a child
when they are fast asleep

children teach us many things like
when to laugh and when to cry
children teach to give of ourselves
when we know not how or why

CHORUS

ADDICTION

The subject I speak of
next, a prediction
we will never ever
abolish addiction

there's many kinds of addiction
so I know I'm not rambling
there's sex and drugs and booze
and one also called gambling

there's many more addictions
around I could name
but for the purpose of this poem
I won't play that game

these addictions are so
very hard to beat
and can knock you down
and off your feet

just when you think
you've come up from the ground
addiction grips you again
knocks you down with a pound

your mind says try to get up
and you'll regret that you did
'cuz I'll hit you harder
take away your kid

you're now in a tighter grip
of this awful thing
and your spouse wants a divorce
off with your ring

now you've lost everything
but god is still giving
let's hope you don't lose
your addiction to living

FOR ELVIRA

She looks like an angel
wings of porcelain white
can cast a devilish spell
with all of her might

don't get me wrong
the spell's not made of danger
it's fraught with delight
for any willing stranger

her message is clear
her motives are pure
for any nice guy
willing to endure

she seeks a lifemate
to take her to ecstasy
not a sometimes mate
who'll say let me be

she doesn't want a guy
whose heart's not all there
she's experienced that once
oh, what despair

she doesn't see
what's in front of her nose
the passion another has
for her grows and grows

she's funny she's witty
she's really quite clever
if only she'll see that
but I fear she'll never

the quality of heart
she has is amazing
but she seems to
pick the wrong guys

to set it to blazing

and so her path
to me seems clear
if she doesn't pick the right man
who is honest kind and sincere
she could end up quite possibly queer

BELIEF

I try to be godlike
I vow to never sin
but when the devil has a go
I feel I cannot win

I try to stand up on my own
the devil I will beat
but then I realize I need help
before I cower in defeat

look up to god, that I must do
he will give me strength
when my courage is in short supply
he will give it length

he will help me in my fight
he will help me win
if I only have the knowledge
to try and let him in

let him take the pain away
let him heal my soul
for the darkness that crept in
took a mighty toll

left me marked with scars not visible
a pain that no one can see
changed me in different ways
but god still knows it's me

he still knows and sees inside
the light that I can't find
he knows that I've lost my way
and it's somewhere behind

what I did not know
or refused to see
god has been there always
just waiting to embrace me

waiting for me to come to him
so he could fix my heart
turn the darkness into light
and let the healing start

and now I am a different person
I have let the lord in
so devil I must say to you
you will never win

BLEEDING LOVE

They say that love will leave you blind
To all broken hearts she left behind
Though she schemed and planned it all
didn't know I was headed for a fall

CHORUS
How was I supposed to know
that you wouldn't go
when I told you no
stop tearing that hole...in my heart

Though your heart says try and try
love can sometimes bleed you dry
just when you think she's ready... for a lawyer
she calls and tells you...I implore ya
to come and give it one more try
but then she goes and bleeds you dry

CHORUS

she calls her friends from all around town
saying "why won't this guy stop making me frown"
she goes to him and pleads her case through
but he won't listen as he says "baby I love you"

soon he gets wise
sees through her disguise
he's just a pawn
in her little game of chess
moved on to the next guy
wearing a much shorter dress

FOREVER

"I'll love you forever"
a phrase that begins it
I'm here to tell you
has a certain time limit

"always and forever"
spoke not knowing cost
the two are in love
it will never be lost

wedding day comes
say hooray
honeymoon follows
time to play

the game of life
we start the next day
seems quite different
now time to pay

for walking the aisle
and saying "I do"
and vowing to spouse
who says "I do", too

then one starts to pan
the long range plan
they didn't sign up for
this enormous tour

down life's rocky road
with one kid, maybe more
starts thinking life sucks
let's hit the floor

and run as far
and as fast as I can
I can't handle this
I'm not a real man

RELATIONSHIP BATTLE

You say that it's over
no longer want me in tow
your heart and mind betray
and one says don't go

the other says goodbye
you want me to leave
which one do you trust
what do you believe

you keep hanging on
can't make up your mind
do you want me to stay
or do you leave me behind

the signals you send
to me are confusing
are you sure that we're through
or are you still using

we started a life
so full of love
but then something happened
I fell from above

and off of my perch
and down to the floor
and you said that you didn't
want me anymore

but I'm still here
still hanging around
because that you haven't
held firm to your ground

I'm still hoping
that we have a chance
because you haven't said
that this is our last dance

if you really and truly
want me to leave
don't send mixed signals
and make me believe

that there's something still for us
that I can hold on to
just be bigger than that
and say that we're through

I'm not grown up enough
to say it needs to end
I've proven before
on me you can't depend

but this game that you play
pull and push my heart
will eventually wind up
tearing both of us apart

one of us must decide
when to pull the plug
and not be drawn in
by yet another hug

instead of leading
the other one on
it's time to say
"see you later, I'm gone"

don't hang on out of fear
and the unknown
it's time that you did it
strike out on your own

show others you can do it
without a life mate
and don't be tied down
to that kind of fate

for a spouse you shouldn't
have to break or to bend
for if you do that
your individuality will end

so go on with your live
without the other one
reclaim yourself
and always have fun

POVERTY

Poverty is something
I can not stand
poverty is something
we should demand

the rich to abolish
for they have the money
but like pooh they won't let us
have their pot of honey

the rich get richer
while the poor have to suffer
under a bridge
without any supper

in very bad places
is where the poor live
because the rich people
don't know how to give

the poor who are lucky
and say, "When we're rich
we'll turn the tables
it'll be time for a switch"

suddenly they turn
from poor into rich
and all of a sudden
therein lies the glitch

they somehow forgot
they were ever poor
and suddenly don't feel
like giving anymore

hypocrite is the name
given to people like these
who now say, "no"
and once begged, "please"

HOW COME

How come I can't feel hopeless
How come I am so souless
How come I can't grieve like others
Cry buckets for their own mothers

How come what I feel inside
doesn't come properly outside
How come pain is easy for others to show
How come I can't cry, I don't know

How come I am all locked up inside
How come I can't find the key, for I have tried
How come I can't feel sorrow and pain
When I know I won't see my mother again

How come my heart is denied from its grieving
How come my mommy never said she was leaving

FOR JOEY

Caught up in a world
that doesn't understand
that he's very different
but others demand

that he plays the game
society wants him to play
but if he does that
he will most surely pay

he will lose who he is
and have to deny what's inside
thinking society shuns him
he must run and hide

even his mother doesn't respect
who he's always been
and hovers around him
like a nosy mother hen

on the computer all day
sometimes can be a trap
has plenty of movies
he's yet to unwrap

for he's waiting to watch them
with someone he can love
instead of watching alone
with chocolate called Dove

he sits at home
and thinks of the past
instead of going outside
and finding something that will last

instead of living
he's only existing
I wish he'd wake up
to what he is missing

the crux of this poem
I see one thing only
is that my dear friend Joey
seems quite lonely

MILITARY BRATS

A military brat is something
I never wanted to be
but by the time I came along
I was victim number three

born into a life
moving from place to place
never knowing where I'd end up
the things I'd have to face

but I somehow adjusted
to my new surrounding
everytime that we moved
got in trouble, then grounding

I was a trooper
with mischief inside
that mischief held tears
that I would expertly hide

losing friends hurt bad
as anyone could plainly see
but the friends had to move
for they were brats just like me

born into the life
that I sometimes blundered
did they feel the same way
I often wondered

life wasn't all bad
or as bleak as I make it
the happiness I showed
I only sometimes faked it

for I got to see
lots of interesting things
that I wouldn't have seen
without airplane wings

I've grown up confused
about moving so much
and missing friends
that I wish kept in touch

but I wouldn't change
the life that I see
before me because
than I wouldn't like me

CRUELTY

Some people say that life is cruel
but they don't have a clue
they don't see the baby going without nourishment
they can't see the bruises behind the walls of the brick tenement

they're oblivious to hunger
cuz they've been fed with a silver spoon
and they can't see the man
dying in the next room

they don't see the drug addict
who's hooked on pills
who's just aching
for his next set of thrills

their lives are actually
going pretty sweetly
why can't others'
lives be managed so neatly

CHORUS

life is cruel
but there's no rule
who will last
who has to fast
who must lie
to get what they need
who must die
so others can feed
they say god is love
but where is he
I'm blind right now
and I can't see

some people have money
so they can buy that yacht
others have to steal to feed

before they get caught

they don't see the hookers
that go to work on the corner
just so they can feed their baby
and wrap them in something warmer

They don't see the beggars
down at the local mission
they're to busy in their boat
with a sign on their door "gone fishin"

CHORUS

FOR CLINT

When a child gets hurt
by powerful words
self esteem gets bruised
by know-nothing little turds

the words stay with
this little lad
puts on a brave face
but inside he's sad

looks for love
and positive reinforcement
when he can't find that
inside what torment

grows into a man
thinking he's less than he is
marries a wife
and has a couple of kids

the wife that he has
he thinks is a soulmate
finds out about his life
and spits out such hate

he tells a friend
about the life he has now
still with his wife
his friend asks how

can you stay with a person
that cuts you down flat
to be really honest
she is not all that

although some you write
come out like a gay larry flint
I'm glad you are my friend
I love you, Clint

GIVE AND TAKE

Just think, a year ago
everything was fine
I had both my parents
everything was in line

then one day I woke up
and my mother died
there was nothing I could say
I hadn't even cried

didn't have time to deal
life played another trick
I was lost without my mom
and then my dad got sick

cancer was the name
of this awful disease
when he knew he had it
I was begging please

rid me of this curse
that keeps leaving me alone
fill my house up now
make it more a home

then my sister came
to rid me of my drought
now that she is with me
I feel I can pout

I'm closer to my sister
much more than before
until all of this happened
I wouldn't even roar

but now that we are closer
than I thought we'd be
I can weep on her shoulder
finally be me

cry all night and day
make my feelings known
for I am very tired of
this bravery I've shown

when my dad goes in the hospital
to get his round of chemo
I am often in the house
getting very emo

when he's feeling bad
and not able for a visit
he tells me stay home
and I feel like shit

I understand his reasons
for not wanting me around
he doesn't want me to see
that his heart is on the ground

he lost his wife and got cancer
all in less a year
I will do my darndest
to fill him with some cheer

happiness and laughter
is the way to keep on winning
when you know you want to frown
just tell yourself keep grinning

life deals you heavy blows
sometimes you want to quit
treat hard times with some oxy
pop them like a zit

hard times are only hard
without the proper question
so I am her to offer
a very helpful suggestion

don't whine and complain
when life isn't what you want
keep beating back the bad times
and you'll always be in front

ODE TO A SICK FRIEND

Though your back it may hurt, and your mind it may crack
keep a reign on that pain, you must kick it back
when life gets you down and you're flat on the ground
just think of me, please turn it around

I am no savior and I ain't no champ
but I'll be your guiding light, I'll be your bright lamp
keep ahead of the crowd, you're already ahead of the game
all the warmth and compassion you show burns bright as a flame

although my life has been sick and my childhood missin'
you show that you care just because you will listen
your life as you told has been no bed of roses
we're better to have known you, when you're in pain we all wipe our noses

we wish and we pray for your suffering to end
we love you so dearly, you are what we call friend
although I have one biologically, I can have no other
I am so proud to say I want you as my brother

FOR MY SISTER

I'm sorry life's dealt
you such heavy blows
you're the last one that needs them
as heaven knows

not all at once
do you need to be hit
the pile grows higher
that's a lot of shit

let's take it slow
easier fights you should pick
try getting hit by a rock
instead of a brick

lessons you learn
are hard to heed
but very often
what you need

so listen and learn
to the lessons they show
for when we do that
we truly do grow

into the people
we most want to be
once we are there
we can truly be free

LIFE'S CRUTCH

Life is my cast
with you as it's crutch
don't live in the past
I've used you too much

When I let you down
please don't frown
your respect isn't earned
when I repeat what I've learned

have to find a new way
in this new role that I play
I must now be a man
and come up with a plan

new obstacles to face
in this great race
to reach the finish line intact
I must realize my impact

on the others that run alongside
to be with me for the ride
I must realize my place
And be careful not to backslide

I must be aware
of what is ahead
turn the blinders off
and try not to be led

astray from my goal
but all that I see
is what I want
it's all about me

the warnings I get
I don't even heed
what is important now
is what you need

wanting is temporary
and then you'll want more
needing is what
will open the door

family is the word
of the day
everything else
can just melt away

for with family around
you have nothing to fear
that's all I want
everyone to hear

PICK UP POEM

It makes me feel teeny
To cry like a weenie
when you're supposed to be a man
and come up with a plan

to dig yourself out of the hole
all you need is a pole
to vault yourself out of the mess
and straight to success

when you're down in the dumps
and life gives you bumps
stick your tongue out, lick all your bruises
look at the less fortunate
and see what he uses

look at others pain
and see what there is to gain
from the inner strength that keeps them alive
draw from them, strive to survive

no one can do
for you what you need
it's all up to you
to go out and succeed

all others can do
is give you the tool
when you reach your success
remember the golden rule

do unto others as
you'd have done to you
and maybe you can help
others reach their goal too

WAR

War is something
that nobody needs
war only ends
when somebody bleeds

the enemies are catagorized
each given a name
but to me they are human
and bleed just the same

the yellows the reds
the enemies are plenty
the winners are happy
when their guns are all empty

cuts and scrapes
and bruises may loom
but the military aren't happy
'til the enemy goes boom

the evils of war
are all around us
most are disguised
by a word they call justice

but where is the justice
in seeing people die
to me it's just cowardice
wrapped up in a lie

just childish playground
bullying stuff
who's army is bigger
who can play rough

don't try to hit me
and then take my toy
I'll come back stronger
and take all your joy

kill your family and loved ones
and everyone around
leave you with nothing
but a spot in the ground

come after you next
with my next round of ammo
when you least expect it
turn around and then whamo

I've got you, you're dead
oh what great joy
now next time they'll know
don't take my toy

but wait, now there is no one
left here to hurt
only me standing
alone on the dirt

the moral of the story
is not hard to escape
PLEASE STOP THE KILLING

TREELESS

A tree keeps blinding light
out of your path
when you are upstairs in your room
trying to do your math

A tree has shade
when there is someone
you are trying to evade
A tree has leaves that help keep you dry
when rain falls down from the night or morning sky

A tree can be made into paper
to write down your thoughts
when you feel you can't find your way
and have become lost

Trees provide fruit
for a growing persons nourishment
instead of junk food
at your local burger joint

trees are full of life
but it's all locked inside
we must find a way
to open it and not let it hide

trees let young ones escape in the night
when angry parents just want to fight
trees provide a good climb
for young ones not wanting crime
trees can be made into a fort
for young ones bad and on report

WHERE

Standing on
the precipice of hell
which way to turn
I never can tell

where do I go
please point the way
life is very complicated
such a difficult game to play

sometimes no rhyme or reason
for things that occur
life happens so fast
often times it's a blur

when you don't have time
to think what do I do
your brain shuts down
those day you often rue

sometimes reacting first
later is when you think
hindsight is perfect vision
when your reasoning takes a drink

of the logic and calmness
you should have had prior
to the moment you decided
when your mind should retire

from when you didn't have everything
clear in your vision
and turned your soft soul
into a hard prison

RACE

We're all the same family
in gods eye
but instead of remembering that
we don't even try

to love one another
and give each other space
in this new millennium
we're still hung up on race

but that game some play
is way out of date
I look in the mirror
and I don't see hate

I see pure love
from white guy to black
but some don't learn
and they just attack

what they learned prior
and now don't understand
we've stopped all the hate
and opened our hand

we no longer fight
the difference in skin
we know there are bigger battles
out there to win

like hunger and poverty
and cancer and aids
and people that kill
with well sharpened blades

what I'm saying is this
look under the face
before you condemn
just because of their race

DEATH

The sound of death
grows so tall
when you are waiting
for the last one to fall

don't know where or when
but you know it'll go down
so you cling to their lives
for the inevitable showdown

the sadness is inside
a terror that no one knows
you're afraid what will happen
if the sadness ever shows

so you keep it locked up
away from people's vision
don't want them to see
your homemade prison

get depressed with each cough
and sniffle they make
you're deathly afraid
who the lord will next take

keep everything guarded
and close to the vest
you know that real soon
you'll be put to the test

losing a loved one
like a family member
leaves you with feelings
you don't want to remember

mourning the day
you lose another
just like that one day
when you lost your mother

GOD STRUGGLE

They say when life gives you lemons
you should make lemonade
when I was born
fate was already made

when momma had me
my fate was sealed
I developed scars
not properly healed

some scars are visible
the rest are not
of this have no doubt
hidden ones hurt a lot

some can't see
the pains they cause others
most get consoled
by their loving mothers

I don't have mine
sadly anymore
to take away the pain
from the heart that people tore

I have deep rooted issues
that will take time to heal
god feeds souls love
will he bring me my meal

will he take away the pain
I have been feeling since birth
the happy one inside
will he finally unearth

do I let him in
do I give him a chance
will he set me free
will he help me dance?

In this next poem I refer to a story. The story that I refer to is a fictional book that I have written, coincidentally with the same name as this poem.

THE GOOD & THE EVIL

The battle between good and evil
is sometimes hard to win
the good ones are beyond reproach
while the evil ones just sin

sometimes good ones slip
and the bad ones aren't all bad
but life isn't all black and white
there is a lot of gray to be had

so as you read this story
ask yourself, "which one am I"
do I always try and tell the truth
or do I just outright lie

although interesting stuff is
in the pages written here
but the moral of the story
is honestly quite clear

the line between good and evil
is something we shouldn't fear
unless the lines get to close
they all of a sudden disappear

MISSING MOM

I try to see my mother
in my minds' eye I browse
for I am like no other
pictures will not rouse

tears fall from my eye
my heart has been abused
no more can I lie
my soul is badly bruised

she was taken from me
on a night moonlit kissed
like a child wanting mommy
her tender touch I missed

even though I plead
she can not come back
what I really need
I do surely lack

she gave me a gift
on the day that I was born
but will my spirit lift
for I am surely torn

presence with me each time
tangibility is not there
come up with a rhyme
so I can show I care

about my mother passing
into a life I cannot see
I'm on my knees to god
please let her be with me

you took love so far away
you kicked me in the dirt
find a way to make you pay
why'd you make me hurt

like the david and goliath battle
ended with a severed head
I'll try and keep my wits about me
on days I wish that I were dead

WAR CRY

War means death
for everyone involved
war is stupid
and nothing's really solved

war pits one side
against the other
instead of looking inside
and realizing he's your brother

war leaves memories
of a time of utter madness
for the ones that survived
it brings great sadness

their lives now filled
with confusion and doubt
what was the war
really about

did the war
bring peace and utter tranquility
or just an excuse
to use a lot of artillery

to show the weaker
that we are strong
why does this war
have to go on so long

why does this fighting
have to happen you ask
I wonder myself
as I pick up a flask

with something inside
to dull all the pain
of the war that rages
inside of my brain

for the war never ended
even though the killing stopped
it's inside of me always
when I saw the enemy dropped

I killed him with my rifle
it happened so fast
now he is gone
and he is the last

I can go home now
to the land of the free
the enemy is dead
I can collect my fee

a job well done
it's a medal I get
but that doesn't wipe away
the feeling of regret

I have for killing
a fellow human being
so now in my nightmares
it's him that I'll be seeing

LIFE SEARCH

Are you confused
are you bemused
my pain is there
but you don't care

out there for all to see
no one really cared about me
when life was passing me by
I was left to wonder why

what my role in life could be
others said open up and see
my life wasn't wasted
my life wasn't trashed
but no one could really see
how it felt inside, my hopes were dashed

no one could see the trauma unfold
no one knew of the secrets untold
no one saw the rage inside
no one could see the little boy trying to hide

and now I'm grown
with a life of my own
my feelings still haunt
this pain I don't want

this desire I'm left with
needing love I hope against hope
someone would notice me drowning
and throw out a very big rope

laughter has always been better than fear
it helps me to hide that big shiny tear
some day I hope to come out of this funk
but unlike my brother I will not be drunk

all I desire are love, kisses, and hugs
but not like my brother, he wanted drugs

the moral of this, so simple and clear
love one another the right way
and pain won't appear

This next poem is going to be in the sequel to my book "The Good & The Evil."

MASKED

Everyone wears a mask
but did you stop to ask
what mine looked like
how it felt
no you didn't
cuz you've never dealt
with the pain
and the anguish
and the secrets
that languish
beneath the soul
that take its toll
on a mind once clear
now filled with fear
take a look inside
and don't try to hide
from the past you deny
for it will never lie
the past keeps coming back
until you find what you lack
you can try to push it under
sweep it beneath the rug
but that's when baggage gets deep
and to heavy to lug
in the end truth comes out
sometimes not planned
when you live your life this way
there's no telling where your heart will land
so take off the mask
show us the real you
so others will know
and finally get a clue
see what you've been up against
how you've had to live
make them take the blinders off
and finally learn how to give

make them feel what you've felt
how you've had to hide
don't let them off easy
don't let it slide
force them to see
what they didn't before
make them realize
and not ignore
for if you continue
with this masked charade
no telling what will happen
who will have paid
if continued in darkness
and forever hid
your face will get dirty
you'll lose the inner kid
the voice that's inside you
screaming to have fun
give it a listen
don't hide and run
so take off the mask
that's all I ask
let others see
that you want to be free
go live your life
without fear and doubt
don't bottle it up
cuz you'll only shout
you'll lose your search
for what you've had before
the inner child
knocking at your door
the door of your heart
left broken and bleeding
by other hearts also seething
for their childhood as well
was taken away
but they chose a bad path
wanted others to pay
should we condemn them
for the pain that they caused us

or look to their heart
as well for justice
for they wear a mask
just like we do
only theirs is kept on
with much tighter glue

UNITED OR DIVIDED

The word united
is a total joke
we have proven
that we're divided folk

we try our best at
improving other land
but fail miserably
in the country that we stand

there's a lot of war
going on so very near
but others need help
so our problems disappear

but how can we fix
what's wrong in other places
when we still have fighting
between our own races

how can we be judge and jury
in other land's trials
when there is so much fighting
within our own lifestyles

there are so many problems
in our own land today
yet we focus on others
and say America, pay

We're too busy worrying
about some other persons mess
and yet we forget the problems
that we must address

The problems I speak of
are too many to mention
but, rest assured
they all need attention

PATH OF SPIRIT

Nobody to love me
everyone is above me
my soul has been hurt
kicked me down in the dirt

been filled up with sin
and I know I can't win
I'm so far behind
my life won't rewind

cuz I know what I missed
and now I am pissed
cuz I can't take back
from the ones who attack

they shove it back in my face
treat me like a disgrace
they sing the same song
and say I did wrong

but they weren't around
to tell me what's right
they didn't stand up
and help me to fight

they just condemn
and then close their eyes
they're too wrapped up
in their own little lies

they have things hidden
that they don't want found
because then they would join me
down in the ground

MOM'S GONE

I thought I heard you clearly
when you said you loved me
but now you are not here
because you are above me

up in heaven
some would say
and I ask myself
do I feel that way

what do I believe
how come you had to leave
I try and hide it to myself
I've had my heart up on the shelf

been hurt too many times
so I don't feel the chimes
ringing in my heart
that says that we're apart

won't let my heart feel
what my mind already knew
that you were already slipping away
before I finally lost you

didn't want to see the truth
that was right before my eyes
so I tried to cover it up
with ignorance and lies

but now I know the truth
and it hurts down deep inside
I don't know what to do
so I let my feelings hide

I don't know what to think
am I glad she's out of pain
or do I need her here
to keep me from the rain

the drops of tears I cry
for the mother that I lost
and caused my heart to break
and my emotions to get tossed

up in the air
and mixed all around
until they're in a jumble
and lying on the ground

trying to pick up the pieces
I'm supposed to be young and agile
but part of me is gone now
and all I feel is fragile

OWN UP

I have a past
I'd like to forget
pictures in my mind
that I do regret

but I can't let go
of all of the sad
for they help remember
some of the glad

you see, each part of my past
does intertwine
so there's no point
to sit there and pine

for the good to come back
and the bad to just fade
it's time that you made peace
with the bed that you've made

own up to what you have done
and all that you are now
for you try to escape
and don't even know how

if you don't own up
your life will be uncertain
and then where do you go
when you face the final curtain

admit what you've done
all your past mistakes
repentance is it's name
that's all that it takes

one final note
and this I do vow
own up to your sins
before your final bow

FRIEND OR FOE

I gotta know
if you're friend or foe
I gotta feel
which one is real

tell me now
should I step back
or do I need to
go on the attack

are you the one
that I call friend
or will this friendship
be the end

of my being
a trusting soul
will your betrayal
take it's toll

and leave me wondering
why I ever took your flack
why did I bother to give
the shirt off of my back

what made me
decide to trust
when you left
me in the dust

I decided
for one more try
but then you told me
one last lie

I thought you'd always
be my friend
but now I see
it has to end

because I found out
that you're my foe
so it's time
for you to go

WHERE TO GO

Don't know where I'm going
damn sure where I've been
down in the murky depths
of a place called sin

not sure how to get out
don't want the devil's wrath
can't seem to get adjusted
down the righteous path

been lost a lot of times
I just seem to stray
just when I think I'm here
I find I've lost my way

every immoral act
I feel I must repent
every single one
from the past to the present

don't know why I did it
what caused the soul to dip
something inside grabbed hold
and caused the moral rip

they say it's always darkest
just before the dawn does hit
and here I am just waiting
in my private hell I sit

for someone to come and save me
and provide the clues I need
to see sunlight and flowers
instead of darkness and weeds

I need someone real bad
to pick me up off of the floor
and finally show me the way
to open up the door

the door before me opens
inside, a revelation
the truth was always there
that god is my salvation

DOWN

Nobody to love me
everyone is above me
my soul has been hurt
kicked me down in the dirt

been filled up with sin
and I know I can't win
I'm so far behind
my life won't rewind

cuz I know what I missed
and now I am pissed
cuz I can't take back
from the ones who attack

they shove it back in my face
treat me like a disgrace
they sing the same song
and say I did wrong

but they weren't around
to tell me what's right
they didn't stand up
and help me to fight

they just condemn
and then close their eyes
they're too wrapped up
in their own little lies

they have things hidden
that they don't want found
because then they would join me
down in the ground

MY FAULT

Brother lies
my fault
mother cries
my fault
baby dies
my fault

I won't write of it all
I'll just write about one
this girl I went to school with knows
it's painful to lose a son

the boy was too old
to be stroller bound
no strength in his legs
now he's in the ground

I could have spoken up
when I saw him one day
shopping with his mother
but in the stroller, he did stay

If I would have said something
on this earth he could stay
but alas I was silent
and with his life he did pay

why do people keep hurtin'
how can I carry this burden
why do people forsake me
how come god doesn't take me

everything
is on my shoulders
it all feels like
heavy boulders

this load that I carry
I wish I could bury

but I feel I can not
so inside it will rot

I carry the guilt
of things that I cause
when other bad happens
I don't even pause

I take on that guilt
as well, you see
for all of the bad
was caused by me

HELP TO HEAL

Segue into life
come back into livin'
but don't forget your past
remember what you've been given

your pain gave you a past
and people need to view it
to make it all work now
all you gotta do is use it

take a look
at what it is you got
and help to fix
the rest of our entire melting pot

what you got to do
is make that pain a teaching tool
to make the others see
and then they won't be a fool

for what you have been through
you must be a guiding light
so turn the pain inside out
and teach the others what is right

some may not understand
they're the ones that need taught the most
so go, reach out your hand
and become their charming host

you must use your past
to brighten the future of others
don't rest on your laurels
or misuse your druthers

you came out of what you were
and although you have scars
now you have to use that pain
and help others reach the stars

REVELATIONS

What you are
is a whole lotta nuthin' to me
there were warning signs
but I was blind, and I just couldn't see

you had another life
you felt that you had to hide
and now things have changed
because I found out, today, that you lied

tell me, what it is
about your life
that made you cheat on
your loving wife

what do you think that
people will say
when they find out
that you betray

you didn't love her
and you never did
all that she wanted
was to have your kid

white picket fence
and a life very plain
and now it's all gone
sucked down and out the drain

the life that I led
wasn't really my choice
afraid to speak up
for I had no voice

the inner me never
cried out vocally
I always accepted
what people did, totally

so before you condemn me
from right where you stand
take a walk, barefoot
inside my homeland

my home is my soul
wrapped in skin and brain
I invite you to slice
cut open a vein

just be sure that you're ready
to hear what I tell
when you take the trip with me
to my personal hell

SOUL SEARCHING

When people see rain
they see a day wasted and spent inside
When I see rain I see the rainbow

When people are ready to start their car and it won't
they see the bill for having to get it fixed
I see a chance to get to know one another

When someone hurts you physically
others see scars and bruises
I see a chance to teach

CHORUS
pain only lasts as long as you let it
a bill isn't paid until you get it
nightmares last little so why even fret it
your soul is forever so lets not forget it

when someone can't sleep
they envision baggy eyes in the morning
I see a beautiful moonlight

when someone doesn't get what they ordered
they never want to go there again
I see a chance to try something new

when the tv goes out before a big game
they complain they're missing something special
I see a chance to tell my wife "let's cuddle"

CHORUS

FINDING MY WAY

I could feel it in my bones, baby
I did something good, maybe
this time will be different from the past
but somehow I don't think that it would last

I've been hurt before and
didn't want it any more
but as time went on, I opened up my eyes
it's time for me to focus on the prize

CHORUS
I believe there's something out there
something we don't understand
instead of just denying
we should open up the hand
I hope I get to know the one
in charge of my fate
for I need to embrace him
before it is to late

I took my pen into my hand
carved my name into the sand
I hope that someone stops and takes a look
at the final product made into a book

the way I lived my life before
didn't open up the door
'til I finally realized that to be free
I had to do it all mainly for me

CHORUS

I need to trust in him
I have no trust for myself
my heart, it has been broken
and my soul put on the shelf

trust is hard for all of us
it's not as easy task

but if we need the strength to trust
all we have to do is ask

life kicked me down, you see
but rather than a frown, I'd be
smart to let it roll right off my back
than let the foolish people just attack

I'm happy with myself right now
because I finally found out how
to let all of the pain and hatred leave
I found a higher power to believe

CHORUS

he has always been there
never fell down on the job
even when we left him
and turned into a slob

when we said we needed
him, he gave a nod
and said come forth and join me
for my name is god

I didn't turn my back on you
I was always there
with you for your greatness
and in your deep despair

I'm glad that you had faith in me and
didn't turn into a rebel
I can surely tell you
you wouldn't like the devil

LOST LOVE

How can it be that
one day they're here
and then the next day
they suddenly disappear

once so lively
you lived without shame
now just a picture
inside of a frame

you held them so close
did you use too much pressure
because now they're just a picture
on top off your dresser

were the secrets that you held
too hard to handle
because now all you have
is on top of your mantle

CHORUS
lost loves
hurt so much
no telling just how
deep inside it will touch
you played the game
and now that you've lost
there's no point
in counting the cost

you stare at the photo
and wonder what changed
could things have been different
what could you have rearranged

what could you have done
to make them stay
but would they really listen
what could you say

how could you make them understand
the loneliness you feel inside
how do you force them to see
something inside of you has died

you had your chance though
and now that it's gone
just leave it alone
it's time to move on

CHORUS

This last poem is for a very dear friend of mine who went up to heaven in January of 2009, and I will miss him very much. Scotty had cerebral palsy, and was unable to communicate without the use of a spelling board.

SCOTTY'S POEM

When losing someone very dear
it's painful in your mind
the gift we must remember is
what the spirit leaves behind

Scotty's spirit left a lot behind
of that I can't deny
so although it's sad to see him go
I cannot weep nor cry

for although the physical being is not here
for us to adore
the spiritual side of Scotty left
all of us much more

the gifts Scotty gave to me
are very quite abundant
of all the things I learned from him
no lesson is redundant

one of the gifts that Scotty gave
is to be tolerant of others
don't look at someone as being different
treat him like your brothers

another gift that Scotty gave
in me can be quite latent
the skill and the ability
to learn to be real patient

I'm sure I learned a lot more from Scotty
than what I've written down
that is why I can not mourn
and I refuse to frown

The most important lesson I learned from Scotty
everyone can learn, from the rich to the meek
you can get your point across
without ever having to speak

www.ingramcontent.com/pod-product-compliance
Lightning Source LLC
Chambersburg PA
CBHW031411040426
42444CB00005B/515